Midnight Editi

SLOTH

COLORING BOOK FOR ADULTS

SMILE SLOTH

Printed in The U.S.A.

TEST YOUR COLOR

1.

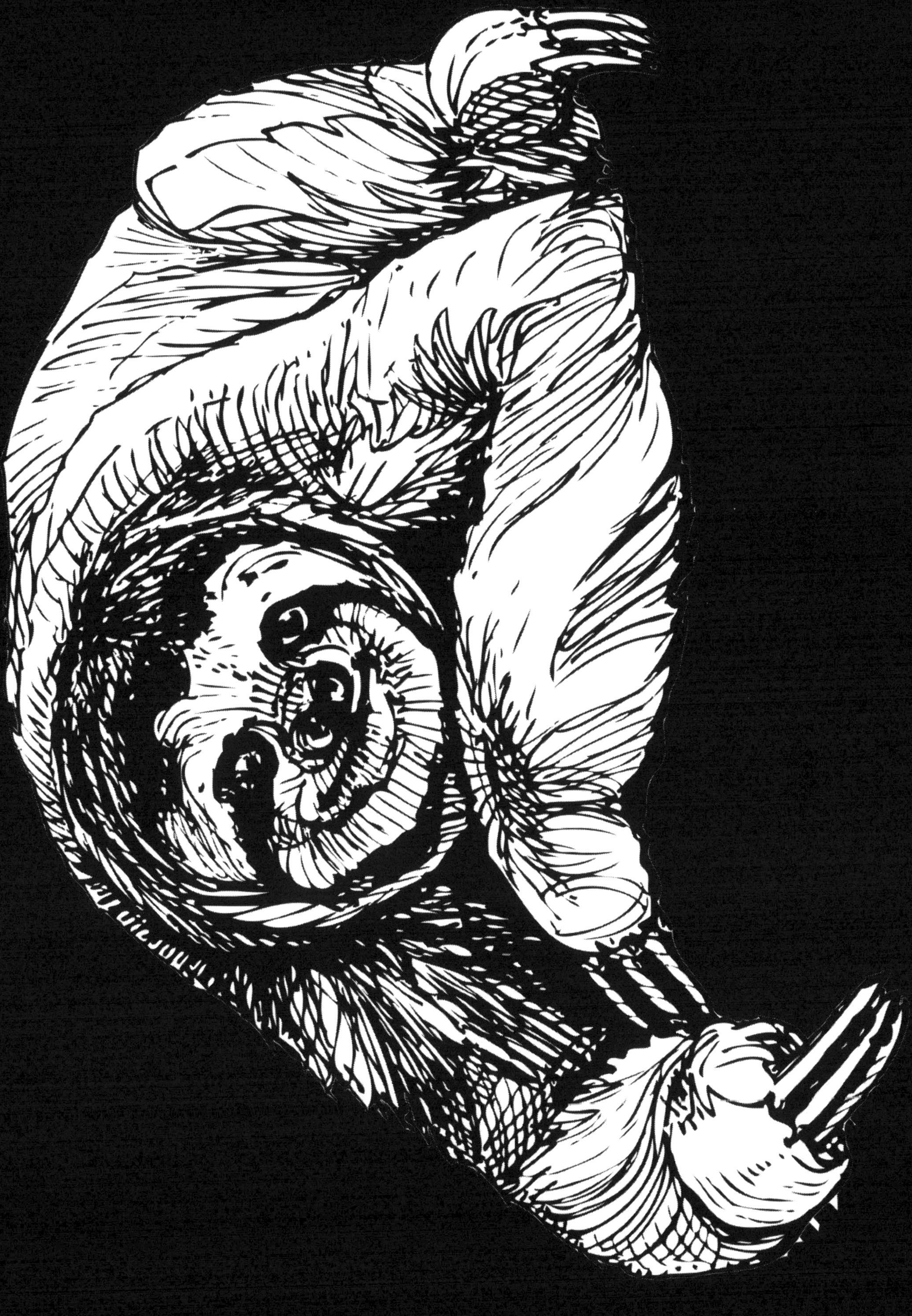

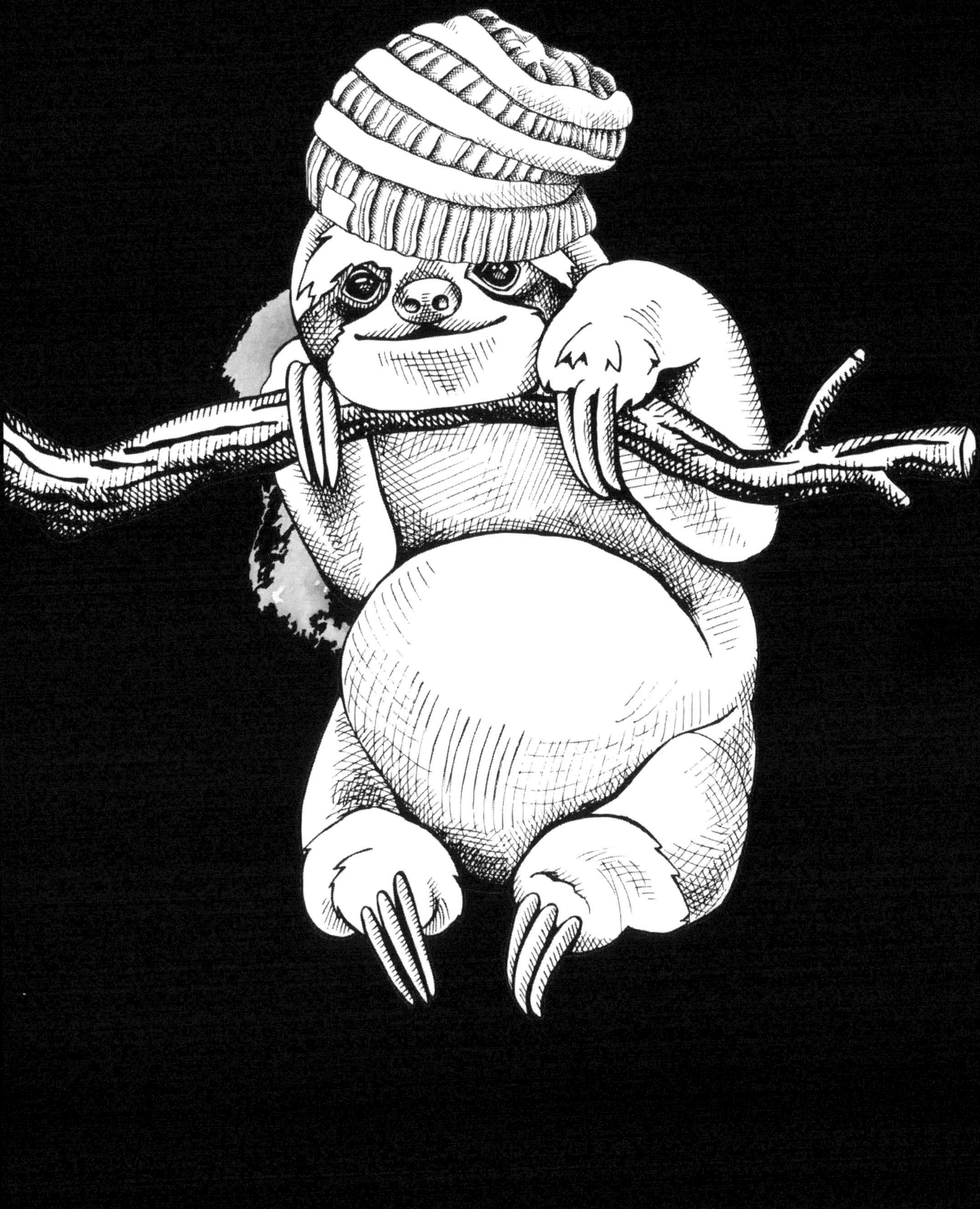

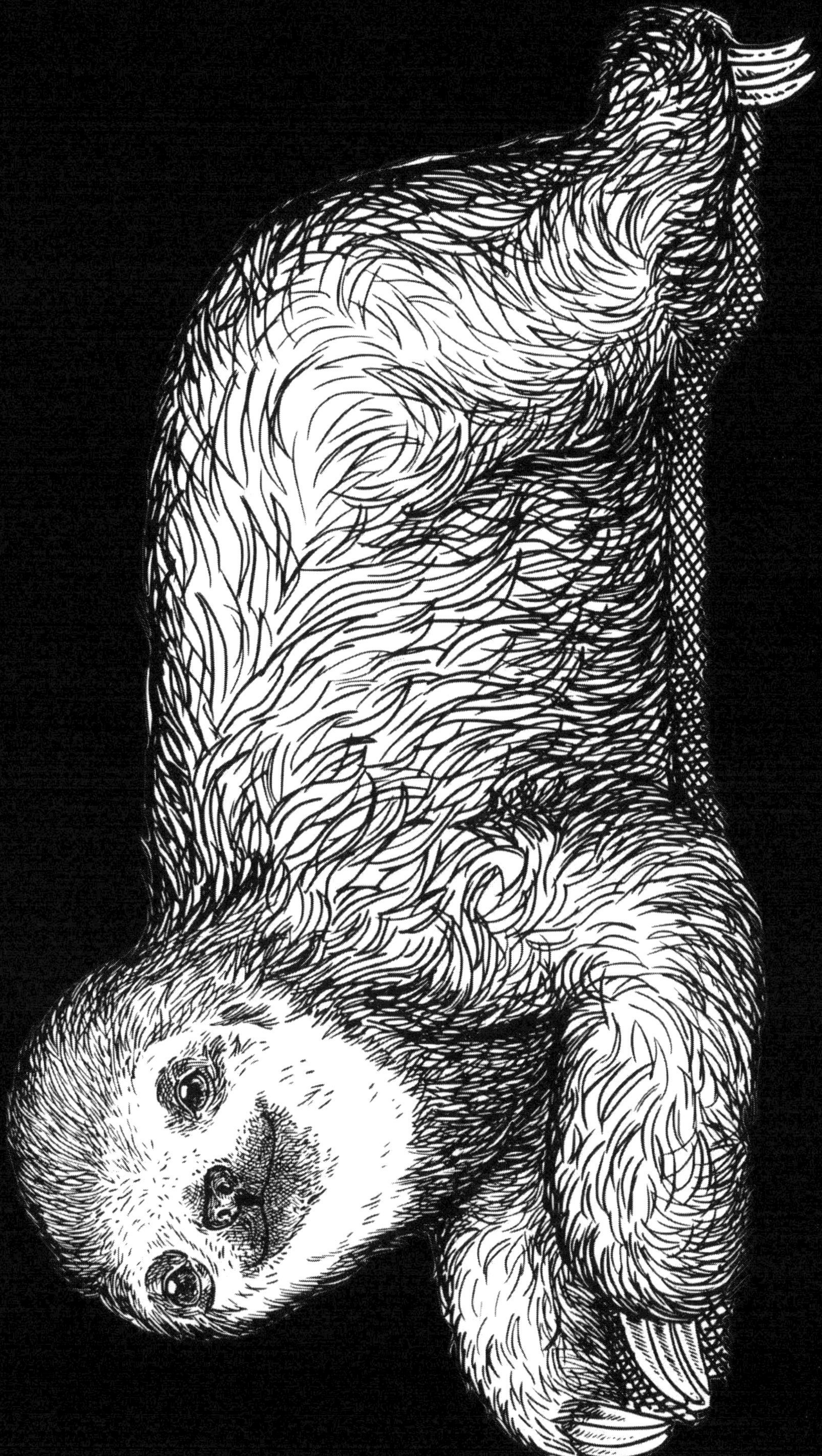

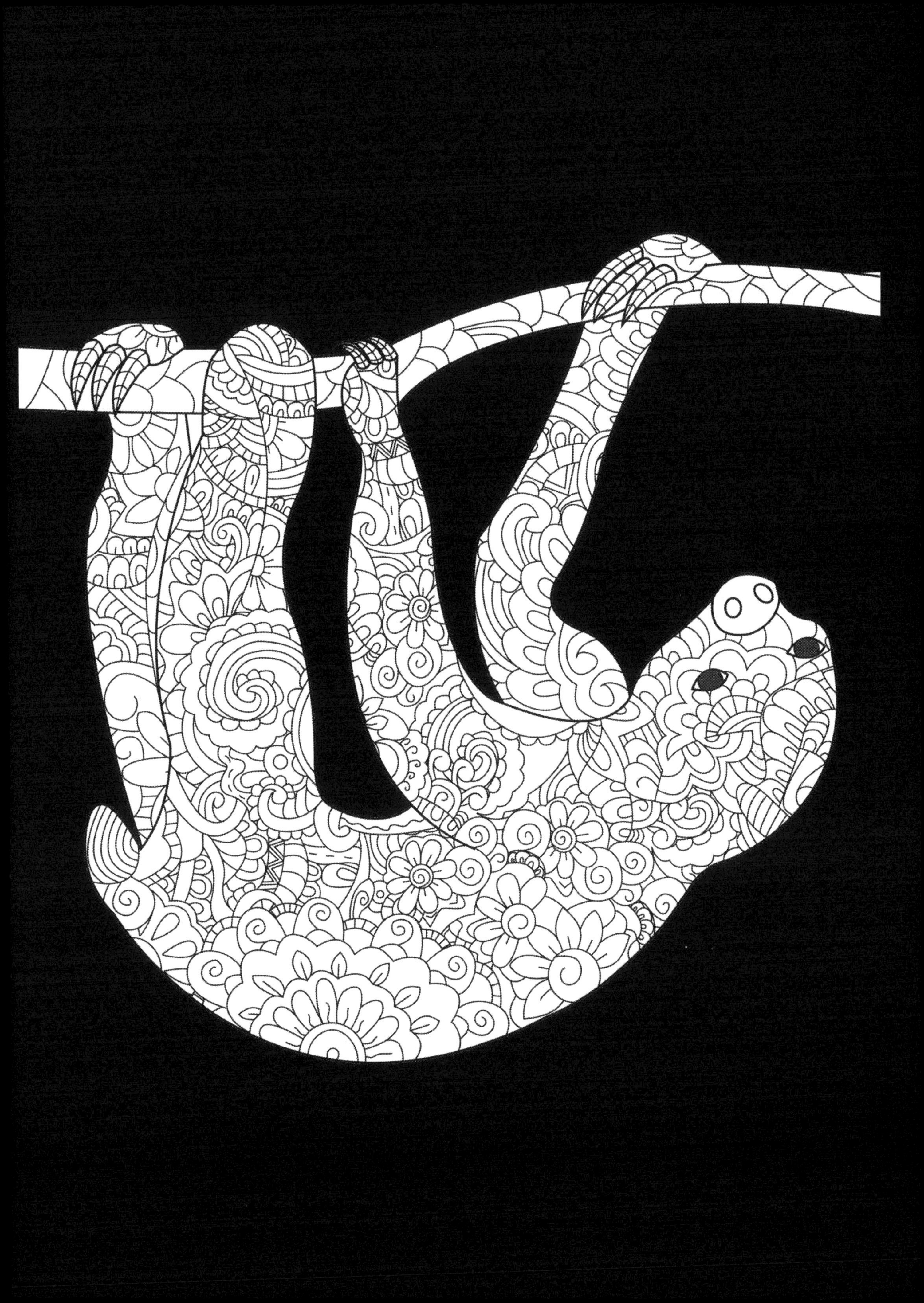

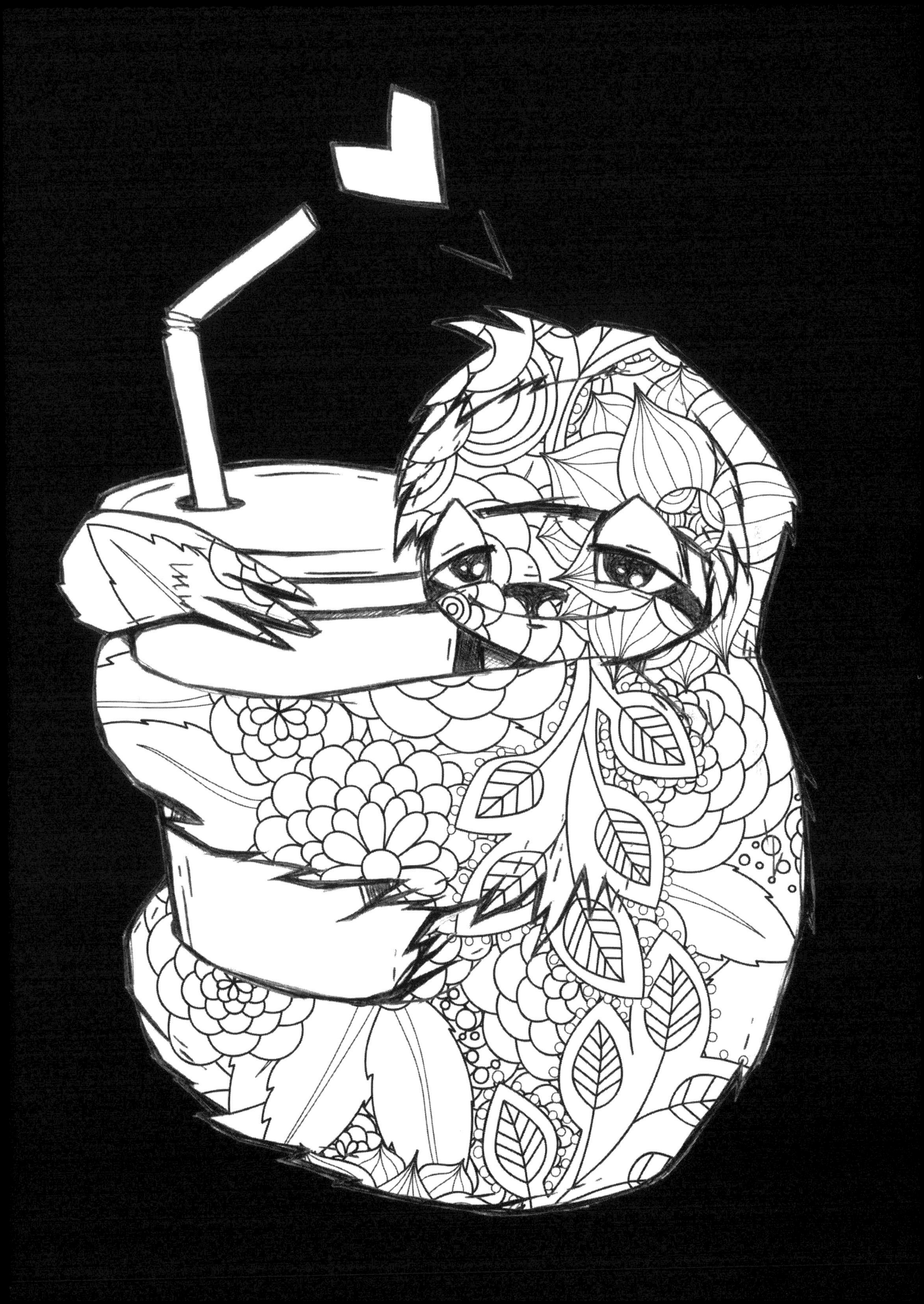

CAMERA

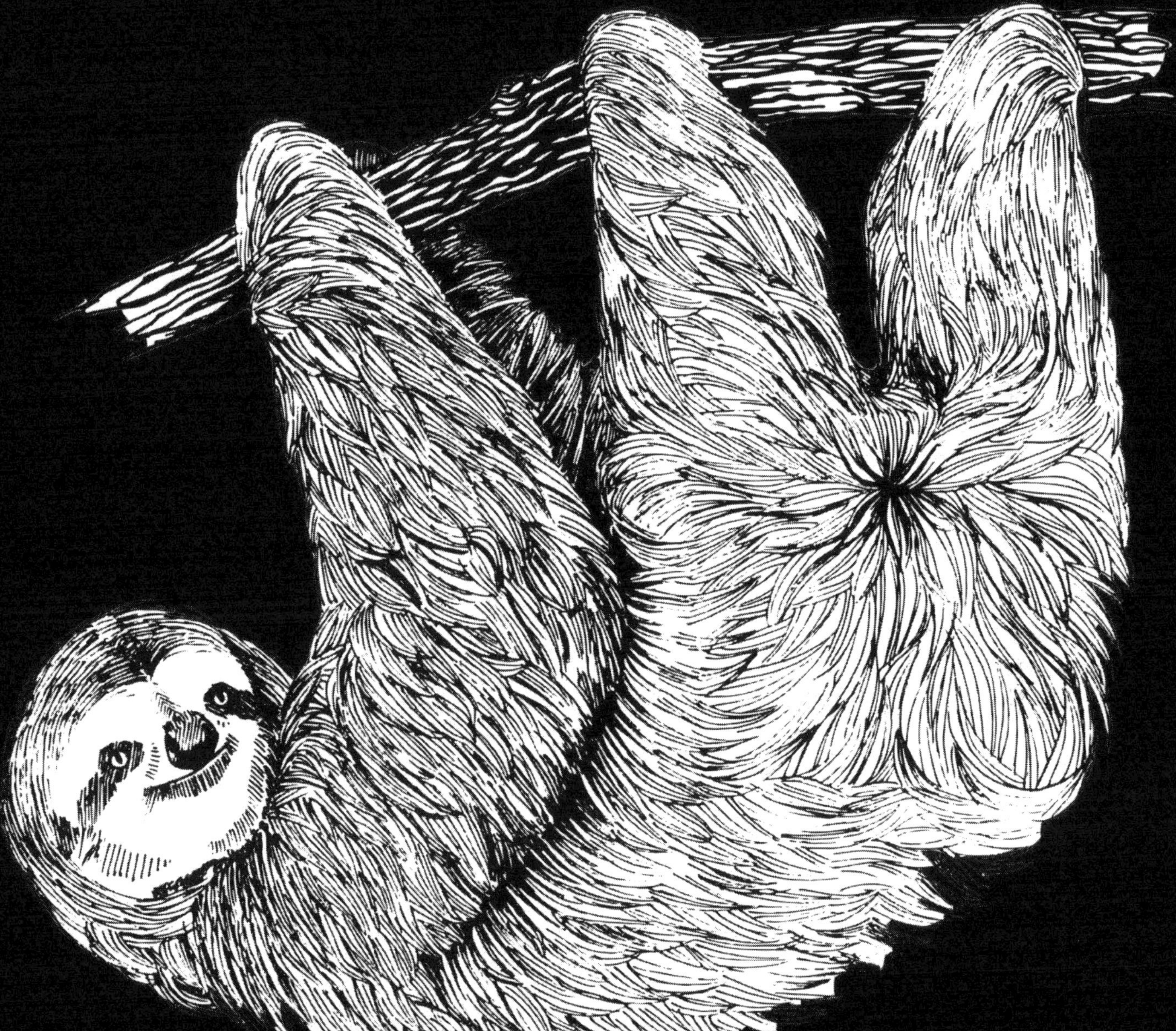